The History of Conservation
Preserving Our Planet

The Formation of the National Park Service

Kaitlyn Duling

Cavendish Square
New York

Published in 2018 by Cavendish Square Publishing, LLC
243 5th Avenue, Suite 136, New York, NY 10016

First Edition

Library of Congress Cataloging-in-Publication Data

Names: Duling, Kaitlyn, author.
Title: The formation of the National Park Service / Kaitlyn Duling.
Description: New York : Cavendish Square Publishing, 2018 |
Series: The history of conservation: preserving our planet | Includes
bibliographical references and index.| Audience: Grades 9-12.
Identifiers: ISBN 9781502631305 (library bound) | ISBN 9781502631312 (ebook)
Subjects: LCSH: United States. National Park Service--Juvenile
literature. | United States. National Park Service--History--Juvenile
literature. | National parks and reserves--Juvenile literature.
Classification: LCC SB486.D85 2018 | DDC 333.72--dc23

Editorial Director: David McNamara
Editor: Kristen Susienka
Copy Editor: Rebecca Rohan
Associate Art Director: Amy Greenan
Designer: Lindsey Auten
Production Coordinator: Karol Szymczuk
Photo Research: J8 Media

The photographs in this book are used by permission and through the courtesy of: Photo credits: Cover Efrain Padro/Alamy Stock Photo; p. 4 Santiparp Wattanaporn/Shutterstock.com; p. 7, 9, 93 U. S. National Park Service; p. 8 Jim David/Shutterstock.com; p. 10 GraphicaArtis/Hulton Archive/Getty Images; p. 14 Maslyar,Brian/Photolibrary/Getty Images; p. 18 Wikimedia Commons/File:Mr. Woodrow Wilson.jpg/Public Domain; p. 21 Corbis/Getty Images; p. 26 Ken Wolter/Shutterstock.com; p. 29 ModernNomads/Shutterstock.com; p. 32 IrinaK/Shutterstock.com; p. 34 Morten Falch Sortland/Moment Open/Getty Images; p. 37 Wim Wiskerke/Alamy Stock Photo; p. 44 ljh images/Shutterstock.com; p. 46 Robert C Nunnington/Gallo Images/Getty Images; p. 52 Kevin Bacher/NPS/Wikimedia Commons/File:Northwest Youth Corps at Mount Rainier National Park 2016 -6I8A7258.jpg/CC BY 2.0; p. 54 Trekandshoot/Shutterstock.com; p. 58 Geoff Livingston/Moment Unreleased/Getty Images; p. 61 Arterra/UIG/Getty Images; p. 64 Al Seib/LA Times/Getty Images; p. 68 U.S. Fish and Wildlife Service Southeast Region/Wikimedia Commons/File:Haywood Community College students planting spruce trees(10344525523).jpg/Public Domain; p. 72 Eric Gregory/Lincoln Journal Star/AP Images; p. 74 Eva Russo/Richmond Times-Dispatch/AP Images; p. 78 Oomka/Shutterstock.com; p. 81 Peter Amend/Image Source/Getty Images; p. 82 YELL 199657: postcard, circa 1960, produced by Intermountain Tourist Supply, Inc., Courtesy National Park Service/Yellowstone National Park Library; p. 85 Christian Science Monitor/Getty Images; p. 90 Education Images/UIG/Getty Images; p. 95 NPS Natural Resources/Wikimedia Commons/File:Biodiversity Youth Ambassadors. NPS Photo. (17679207338).jpg/CC BY 2.0; p. 98 John and Lisa Merrill/Corbis/Getty Images.

Printed in the United States of America

TABLE OF CONTENTS

NATIONAL
PARK
SERVICE
Department
of the Interior

Introduction

The smell of fresh flowers, the sound of rollicking streams. The humid air of the Everglades. The deep, wide allure of the Grand Canyon. Without the National Park Service (NPS), these and hundreds of other national treasures may not be accessible. In fact, without the organization, they might not exist at all. For more than one hundred years, the NPS, an agency of the United States federal government, has managed each national park, as well as national monuments, battlefields, preserves, seashores, lakeshores, and other properties. Additionally, the NPS maintains the National Register of Historic Places, providing grants that help to identify, evaluate, and protect historic places. More than 275 million people visit national parks each year, and that number continues to grow. It is the job of the National Park Service to safeguard the lands that are so loved by US citizens, as well as visitors from around the globe.

Understanding the NPS

The mission of the National Park Service, according to the agency, is to preserve "unimpaired the natural and cultural resources and values of the National Park System for the enjoyment, education, and inspiration of this and future generations. The Park Service

Opposite: This sign welcomes people to the NPS. The NPS is a bureau of the US Department of the Interior, a cabinet-level agency.

cooperates with partners to extend the benefits of natural and cultural resource **conservation** and outdoor recreation throughout this country and the world." It partners with more than 150 nonprofit associate groups, the National Park Foundation, and more than seventy-one cooperating organizations in order to ensure that animals and wildlife are conserved and the nation's parks are properly funded and protected for future enjoyment.

The Importance of National Parks

National parks not only serve as gathering places for recreation, but they are valuable educational tools, stunning examples of natural beauty, and homes for some of Earth's most precious creatures. The parks contain giant sequoias, the world's largest. Together, they have over 18,000 miles (28,968 kilometers) of hiking trails, at least 247 species of threatened or endangered plants and animals, and almost 27,000 historic structures. In the national parks, you can find over 400 miles (644 km) of mapped caves. You can encounter the world's largest carnivore—the Alaskan brown bear. And you can tilt your head back to witness the peak of the tallest mountain in North America, Denali, which reaches 20,310 feet (6,190 meters) into the air. The parks are spread out across the United States, and they each have their own unique character.

The parks, though they reach from the deserts of the far West to the southern coastlines of Florida, are meant to be enjoyed by all people. That includes US citizens and global travelers, who help promote these sites by visiting them each year. Though their beauty is often highlighted, the parks are much more than a pretty view. They are protected regions for plants and wildlife, educational destinations for children and families, and centers of recreation.

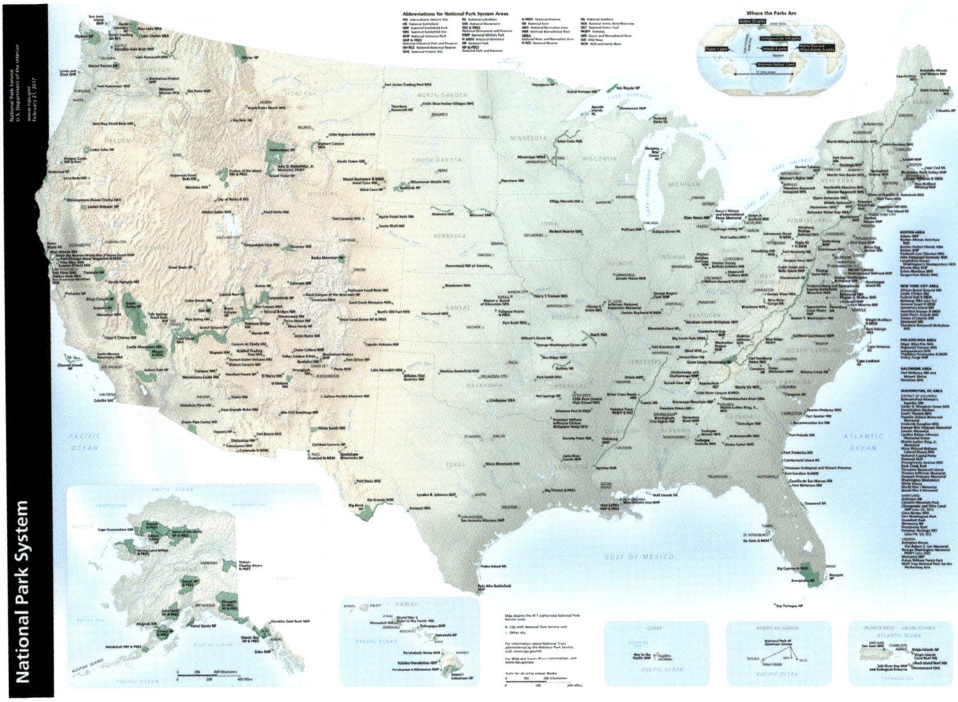

As this map shows, the National Park System is vast, stretching out across the entire United States, including Alaska and Hawaii.

What's more, the NPS covers not only the national parks, but it also holds authority over many monuments and battlefields. The NPS even controls many parts of the National Mall—and its iconic monuments, memorials, and acres of green space—in Washington, DC!

The history of the NPS is woven through with politics, bureaucracy, conservation, love for the outdoors, and more. It is compelling, a little dramatic, and, ultimately, beautiful. The NPS emblem, authorized in 1951, includes three "prongs" of NPS protection: historic and archaeological resources represented by the arrow; recreation and scenery represented by the mountains and water; and natural resources represented by the bison and sequoia tree. These three major categories form the overarching umbrella of protection that the NPS holds over much-loved lands.

Parks belonging to the NPS house beautiful scenery and diverse wildlife. Here, an Alaskan brown bear wades in the water.

Fighting for the NPS

Today, more than ever, it is important that people have a broad understanding of the National Park Service and a thorough knowledge of the valuable work the agency does. With more than 22,000 employees and 340,000 Volunteers-in-Parks (VIPs), the NPS covers a significant amount of ground. In fact, VIPs donate around eight million hours of service each year! However, the parks aren't simply staffed by the khaki-wearing **rangers** of the public imagination, those who are entrusted with caring for the parklands. Different types of workers, each with their own interests and duties, keep the parklands running smoothly. They care for the trails, watch over historic and prehistoric structures, and keep delicate ecosystems in balance. Ferocious Alaskan brown bears, incredible giant sequoia trees, and America's deepest lake are all under their **purview**. For NPS workers and VIPs, caring for our planet is their priority and way of life.

Today, the work that those employees do on behalf of the national parks has never been more important. When the NPS was created, and for decades in between, these treasured lands

NPS rangers provide education to visitors of all kinds. Here, a ranger in North Cascades National Park discusses climate change.

have been at risk. Now, tightened budgets, maintenance backlogs, partisan politics, and environmental stresses all weigh on the parks, and on the NPS, on a daily basis.

Over the past one hundred years, there have certainly been disagreements and challenges related to park management, wildlife conservation, and park use. But the parks remain open to all. Journalist Heather Hanson puts it this way: "Why else should Americans … fully fund the park service? Because by caring for parks we care for *ourselves*. Because they remind us who we are and who we want to be." Hanson's words resonate with special strength today. By reflecting on the history of the NPS and looking toward its future, we have the opportunity to protect one of the nation's most loved and valuable **public goods**, securing the availability of the parks for future generations to enjoy.

RANGER NATURALIST SERVI
NATURE WALK
FIELD TRIPS
CAMP FIRE-
PROGRAMS
NATURE TALK
YELLOWSTONE
NATIONAL
PARK
U.S. DEPARTMENT
OF THE INTERIOR
NATIONAL PA

1

Starting the NPS

The history of the National Park Service begins long before the NPS was formally created in 1916. To truly understand and appreciate its founding and continued existence, one must first have a base understanding of the events of the nineteenth century that led to its eventual creation.

Early History

Its story begins in Yellowstone National Park, or at least in the land that would become Yellowstone. Located in modern-day Wyoming, with portions stretching into Montana and Idaho, the 3,472-square-mile (8,992-square-kilometer) wilderness area features hot springs, geysers, animals, plants, waterfalls, and even a petrified forest. It is larger than the states of Rhode Island and Delaware combined. Today, over 3 million visitors traverse the park each and every year. In 2016, visitation topped 4.2 million.

Opposite: Since the beginning of the NPS, the agency has advertised its parks and services through artistic posters. This poster is from 1938.

Without designation as a national park, and without the help of the National Park Service, millions of people may never have had the opportunity to experience Yellowstone the way they can today.

In the early 1800s, Native American tribes, as well as some fur traders and trappers, inhabited the area that would become Yellowstone National Park. Between 1804 and 1806, explorers Meriwether Lewis and William Clark passed near Yellowstone on their famous expedition to chart new lands. Throughout the 1800s, other organized expeditions also attempted to explore parts of Yellowstone. Some were successful, while others failed, yet each one had stories of fast rivers and hot geysers. However, these stories were often treated as "tall tales" by people back at home. Finally, in 1827, the first accounts of Yellowstone were printed in the *Gazette of the United States & Daily Advertiser,* a publication out of Philadelphia, Pennsylvania. However, there wasn't much to gain from the area in terms of gold or fur, so it remained largely unexplored through the first half of the nineteenth century.

After gold was finally discovered just northwest of the parklands in 1862, expeditions became more common. Accounts were published in papers up and down the East Coast. Curiosity eventually took hold of people.

One popular myth says that in 1870, explorers sat around a campfire right at the meeting point of two beautiful rivers. Behind them were towering cliffs. While recounting their adventures, they realized the land needed to be preserved, and they were effectively the first people to come up with the idea for Yellowstone National Park. It wasn't until 1871, however, that the first government-sponsored exploration, the Hayden Expedition, headed out. This group comprised members of the US Geological Survey, painters, and adventurers.

In a time before the internet, before cell phone cameras, and long before video, the government and the public were finally able to get "proof" of the stories coming out of Yellowstone. This largely came from innovations such as the camera, as well as sketches and paintings done by expedition members. The geysers, the rivers, and the extreme and majestic beauty were all proven to be real. Additionally, impassioned pleas were made to Congress by explorers, writers, and artists who wanted to protect the area.

After hearing this, Congress acted fast. Senate Bill 392 was introduced in December 1871, suggesting that the area be set aside for public purpose rather than private use. In 1872, the Yellowstone National Park Protection Act, signed by President Ulysses S. Grant, created the first national park. Through this legislation, 2 million acres (809,371 hectares) were set aside as public lands, unable to be sold, settled, or occupied. Yellowstone was put under federal control, specifically under the Department of the Interior.

Crafting the Bill and Making a Park

In its first years, the park existed at no cost to the government. With an unpaid superintendent, no basic structures, and no law enforcement rangers, Yellowstone operated with little to no resources. In fact, those who were interested in visiting the park had very few options for traveling there. After arriving by train in either Bismarck, Dakota Territory, or Corinne, Utah, they could travel into the park by bumpy stagecoach. Alternatively, travelers could take a 3,100-mile (4,988 km) steamboat ride from St. Louis, Missouri, to the Montana Territory—and then take a bumpy stagecoach. In the first five years, fewer than five hundred tourists decided to make the journey into Yellowstone.

Slowly but surely, along with some advances in travel, the number of visitors climbed. By 1879, annual visitors had grown to over one thousand. A one-story, sod-covered building served as

Impressive geysers and ambling bison dot the rolling fields of Yellowstone National Park.

the "hotel" in the Mammoth Hot Springs area. The first national park was a far cry from the expansive, recreation-focused, visitor-friendly areas available today.

Another jump in visitors didn't come until the Northern Pacific Railroad reached Yellowstone in 1883, making a much easier and more attractive form of travel available. Of course, the rail trip was expensive, even for middle-class travelers, and even though a couple of new hotels had sprouted up near the park by this time, visitors were still obligated to take a dust-covered stagecoach from the train station in Cinnabar, Montana, to the park's Gardiner entrance, located over 3 miles (5 km) away. As rail lines increased, so did accessibility to the West and, consequently, visitation to Yellowstone. Soon, this would open up opportunities for even more parks.

Before Yellowstone

While Yellowstone was the first official national park, several other places have tried to lay claim to that designation over the years. Hot Springs, an area in Arkansas, has been listed by some sources as the first national park. It was set aside in 1832 to preserve and distribute hot water. Its use was utilitarian in nature, and therefore it did not earn the official title of national park. Many years later, in 1921, Congress finally established Hot Springs as a national park in its own right.

Similarly, Yosemite was recognized as a state park in 1864, when President Abraham Lincoln signed the Yosemite Grant Act. This bill established Yosemite Valley and Mariposa Grove as protected wilderness areas within California. Many view this event as the actual birth of the National Park System, as it was the first time in US history that any land was designated for public use (not just utilitarian use). In 1890, Congress turned Yosemite into a national park, a designation it still holds today.

President Woodrow Wilson signed the Organic Act on August 25, 1916, officially creating the National Park Service.

them. To motorists, this made the road trip—especially to the national parks—integral to the American experience. Park visitors were helped by new guidebooks and "a plethora of **parkitecture**," hotels, and other infrastructure that served the public within the natural settings of the parks. This was the time period in which the national parks developed the look and feel they have today, especially in terms of buildings, trails, and amenities. This was also the period in which rangers became ubiquitous within the parks.

Men and women, young and old, have held the much-loved ranger position, both seasonally and year-round, since the founding of the NPS. They serve as both educators and interpreters, as well as a host of other roles and duties. The first rangers' job descriptions were formulated in the early 1900s. At that time, characteristics of a good ranger included "good character," "sound physique," and the ability to "ride and care for horses." A ranger had to "be a good shot with rifle and pistol" and was even expected to have a range of simple cooking skills.

The NPS and the Great Depression

Unlike the technological advancements, increased travel, and prosperity of the NPS's early years, the 1930s were a tough time, not only for the National Park Service but for the whole country. The Great Depression hit the United States hard, knocking families, as well as government agencies, into economic uncertainty. These were times of great upheaval, and the National Park Service was not shielded from that. Two important events, as well as one notable new project, defined the era and helped keep the parks afloat.

fact!

"Parkitecture" is a well-recognized architectural style, also known as "National Park Service Rustic." This style developed in the early-to-mid twentieth century as the NPS worked to create buildings that blended in with their natural environments without interrupting the surroundings.

President Franklin D. Roosevelt issued two executive orders in 1933 that had significant impacts on the NPS. These orders transferred parks and monuments previously under the authority of the War Department to the National Park Service. The NPS also received the national monuments held by the Forest Service, as well as nearly all monuments created after that date. Additionally, the NPS inherited the parks, monuments, and public buildings within Washington, DC. Previously, these were managed by a separate office located in DC. The reorganization greatly expanded the holdings of the National Park Service and made the role of historic preservation a primary job of the agency.

Two years after the reorganization, the Preservation of Historic Sites Act drew upon the newly expanded historical preservation mission within the NPS. Through declaration of "a national policy to preserve for public use historic sites, buildings and objects of national significance for the inspiration and benefit of the people of the United States," the act gave duties to the NPS, as well as the secretary of the interior, that included conducting surveys of historic properties, doing research, and restoring and maintaining historic properties.

One of the hallmark emergency programs started in the 1930s was the Civilian Conservation Corps (CCC), a work-relief program. This bold project was spearheaded by President Roosevelt himself, as part of his New Deal, a plan that proposed to get Americans back to work and help lift the country out of the Great Depression. Roosevelt hoped to put people to work and help families struggling with homelessness, hunger, and more, while also improving the parks and the acres of natural areas that had been destroyed by industrialization, deforestation, flooding, and the **Dust Bowl**. The project was so important to the president and his platform that he proposed it to his staff just hours after taking the oath of office in 1933.

fact!

Though women weren't allowed in the official Civilian Conservation Corps, First Lady Eleanor Roosevelt started her own initiative that mirrored the program. Known as "she-she-she" camps, Eleanor's version put 8,500 homeless women to work in ninety camps across the country.

In Cochetopa National Forest, Colorado, CCC workers took part in reforestation projects, like planting acres of ponderosa pine trees.

In April of that year, Roosevelt signed the Emergency Conservation Work Act, mandating the establishment of the CCC, and just five days later, twenty-five thousand men had signed up for the CCC. However, women were barred from participation.

The program targeted unemployed men, ages eighteen to twenty-five, most of whom came from struggling families. They lived full-time in camp locations, most of which were within national parks, and worked five days a week for a wage of thirty dollars per month. Twenty-five of those thirty dollars were sent directly to their families, ensuring that those at home were receiving significant benefits from the program.

> *fact!*
>
> **Even though they professed themselves to be a nondiscriminatory organization, the CCC did not give a fair share of work to men of color. This was a significant problem in the South. By 1936, about 10 percent of the CCC was made up of black workers.**

Wearing blue denim work shoes, these men were dispatched to the parks after thorough physical exams and two weeks of physical conditioning that prepared them for the manual labor they would encounter. During the course of the program, workers developed hundreds of miles of trails and roads, constructed thousands of lodges, visitor centers, employee houses, and restrooms, and worked on disease control. They planted more than two billion trees (as well as shrubs and native plants) and worked on challenging projects like erosion mitigation and firebreak construction, helping to preserve natural resources for the future. Additionally, bridges, campgrounds, and fire towers were built.

Native Americans, African Americans, veterans, and residents of nearby rural areas were all integral to the work. They all committed themselves to each task. They lived in camps close to monuments or within the parks themselves. By the fall of 1934, there were 102 camps in national parks and at monument sites, as well as over two hundred camps within state parks.

Without the CCC, the Appalachian Trail may never have reached completion, and the sections of the trail that CCC workers built have stood the test of time, never needing rerouting. CCC workers ran telephone lines and electrical lines in the Grand Canyon. Amphitheaters and entire sewer systems were built. The number of projects completed by workers at these camps is truly remarkable.

According to estimations by the National Park Service, the work that was done by the CCC in the national parks and monuments was equal to more than $9 million in improvements. Over its nine-year run, the Corps employed more than two million men, worked within ninety-four national parks and monuments, constructed 711 state parks, and resulted in 138,000 miles (222,089 km) of new trails and roads.

Roosevelt's administration and the general public were pleased with the outcomes of the program, though some did perceive drawbacks. Conservationists weren't happy with the amount of construction, noting the change in landscape that buildings and trails brought with them. Amid all the disruption and building within the parks, some scientists cried out about a lack of biologists on staff.

Though the CCC certainly wasn't a perfect program, it did have a lasting impact on the parks and monuments. Today, you can still enter the buildings, walk across the bridges, and hike the trails that were built by the Corps workers. Additionally, the workers' engagement with the parks didn't end when they went home. They were able to share stories with their families, friends, and neighbors, strengthening the public's perception of the national parks and the NPS. Conservation and preservation became familiar in more "mainstream" culture, and middle-class and economically disadvantaged communities were suddenly talking about the parks as a valued public good.

World War II

The whirlwind of improvements made within the parks all came to a screeching halt, along with everything else in the country, on December 7, 1941. With the Japanese bombing of Pearl Harbor, the United States entered World War II, and suddenly, everything changed. The CCC was dissolved. The NPS budget was sharply cut. Park rangers left the parks in droves, heading straight into the military, and all park development and expansion stopped. The parks remained standing, but the rush of tourists and employees all but dried up completely. In fact, between 1941 and 1942, visits to the national parks dropped a full 55 percent.

During the four years of American involvement in the war, the parks' resources were heavily targeted. Timber, mineral deposits, grazing lands, salt, and much more were desirable resources during the austerity years of the war. Almost everything was in short supply, and the NPS, as well as the individual parks, was constantly on the defense to protect their lands. Some regions were utilized as training grounds for paratroopers and ski troops. The hotel within Yosemite became a navy hospital. There was even a proposal to quarter enemy aliens inside national park grounds, though it was never approved or enacted. By the end of US involvement in the war, the parks had adapted somewhat to suit the needs of the time, but they were ready to get back to their original purpose—recreation, education, conservation, and preservation—rather than housing soldiers or cutting down trees to help the war effort.

Moving Forward in the 1950s

As conditions in the parks declined, the American public took notice, and turned to the media to voice their consternation. In 1953, *Harper*'s magazine included a column titled "Let's Close the National Parks," that detailed the decline of the parks and the lack of available funding needed to fix broken toilets, dirty campgrounds, and trash-filled picnic areas. More newspaper articles followed. Conrad Wirth, who directed the NPS from 1951 to 1964, took notice. He then decided to take action.

Wirth knew that by the 1950s, nearly all park visitors were arriving by car. In his pitch to Congress, he appealed to both the automobile-related industries and the car-loving American people. Partnering with companies like Sinclair Oil Corporation, Phillips Petroleum, and Standard Oil Company, as well as the American Automobile Association, Wirth painted a picture of the new American park-going family. This was a family that traveled to the parks on new interstate highways, driving away from the suburbs and straight into the national parks. He appealed to Congress to fund a ten-year program called Mission 66. It would include upgraded facilities, more staff, and better management of resources, with an aim to reach these goals by the fiftieth anniversary of the NPS in 1966. The three prongs of Mission 66 were planning, technology, and architecture. All-new picnic areas, amphitheaters, utility lines, visitor centers, trails,

The official NPS emblem was authorized on July 20, 1951. Today, it is widely used on signs and publications.

roads, campgrounds, and observation towers would be erected. Thankfully, Congress agreed to Wirth's vision.

Through its integration, over one hundred visitor centers were installed within the parks. This gave rangers a home base for their interpretation work and provided space for gift shops, films, restrooms, and museum displays. There were purely recreational additions, too, including skating rinks, stables, and ski lifts.

Over a ten-year period, Congress put more than $1 billion into Mission 66. Some have called this period the "golden age" of the National Park Service. Citizens were visiting parks and investing in them, and members of Congress were doing the same. This plan ultimately helped mold the parks into what we know today.

Growth and Change

After a firm foundation for park investment was set with Mission 66, the 1960s and 1970s would prove to be times of immense growth and change, especially on a legislative level, for the National Park Service. The wave of "acts" began in 1964 with the Wilderness Act, a policy of securing wilderness areas. Through this act, Congress also established a national wilderness preservation system and provided for additional legal protection for certain park areas being threatened with development. With this legislation, Congress hoped to protect wilderness areas for future public use. Similarly, the National Historic Preservation Act of 1966 required all historical parks to be entered in the National Register of Historic Places. This meant that decisions by the National Park Service, such as the demolishment of historic structures or changes to the landscape, would become subject to review by state historic preservation officers. Archaeologists, historians, and other preservation specialists cheered this legislation, as it meant that the cultural resources industry was expanded and more jobs would become available to them.

Two 1968 acts, the Wild and Scenic Rivers Act and the National Trails System Act, greatly expanded the diversity of holdings under the National Park System. In the years that followed, many rivers and adjacent lands were added to the purview of the NPS under the Wild and Scenic Rivers System. Along with rivers and river segments, national scenic trails and national recreation trails accessible to urban areas were added to the management load of the NPS. The National Trails System Act designated two national scenic trails: the Appalachian Trail and the Pacific Crest Trail, on opposite sides of the country, and left room for expansion.

To assist with the growing number of NPS locations and the ever-growing population of tourists within them, the Volunteers in the Parks Act of 1969 created the volunteers-in-the-parks program that still exists today. Before this act, the NPS was unable to easily and effectively utilize volunteer help within the parks. Each year since the act was passed, more and more people have volunteered within the country's national parks, and their help has been extremely beneficial in both large and small ways.

The Seventy-Fifth Anniversary of the NPS

Leading up to its seventy-fifth birthday in 1992, the National Park Service saw a few more changes and growth moments heading its way. Though the millennium was fast approaching, Congress didn't intend to slow down its NPS legislation train. The Alaska National Interest Lands Conservation Act of 1980 added over 47 million acres (19 million ha) of Alaskan land to the NPS, more than doubling the size of the system. More than viable lands

Vast protected areas—like the Smoky Mountains, pictured here—provide countless opportunities for visitors to explore and engage with nature on a grand scale.

for visitation, the act increased the size of protected wilderness areas, expanding land management responsibilities for the NPS and putting a sizable amount of land under its protection and care.

Following these additions, the National Park Service began to prepare for its seventy-fifth anniversary. The birthday was celebrated through merchandise like pins, commemorative books, and celebrations at several parks. Of note is a special seventy-fifth anniversary foldable knife that is now sought after by serious collectors. To mark the occasion in a more formal and useful way, in 1991, the NPS held a symposium (public meeting) in Vail, Colorado, that included several hundred participants.

At the symposium, the group analyzed problems facing the agency and intended to make recommendations that would help set the stage for the twenty-first century. Six strategic objectives came out of the meeting: resource **stewardship** and protection, education and interpretation, access and enjoyment, professionalism, science and research, and proactive leadership. These objectives, along with other findings and suggestions, were published and forever after known as the Vail Agenda. This document reiterated needs that had been expressed in the State of the Park Report of 1980, which outlined environmental and human threats to the parks, and also expressed new concerns, urgently recommending that park management ground itself in scientific research. This symposium and the resulting document gave the National Park Service a platform from which to dive headfirst into the twenty-first century.

Mapping the National Parks

The NPS's Ten Most-Visited National Parks in 2015

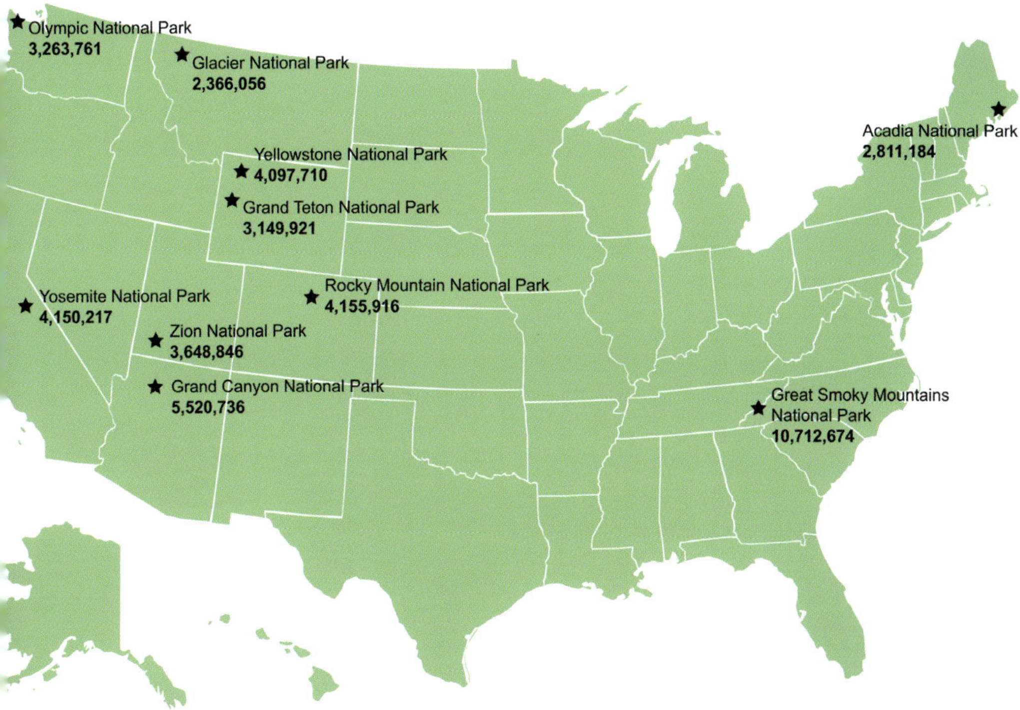

2

The NPS from the 1990s to Today

As the sun set on the seventy-fifth birthday of the National Park Service in 1992, park officials, workers, volunteers, and visitors turned toward the years to come. Before they knew it, there would be another milestone—the new millennium. As the year 2000 crept closer, everyone wondered and worried about big changes that might take place when the clock struck and the year moved forward: Would there be natural disasters? Would technology stop working? Those in the NPS administration may have had some of the same worries, but they stayed focused on the challenges at hand. The 1990s, which were generally a time of economic prosperity for many in the United States, did present new challenges for the NPS and the parks under its care.

Changes and New Initiatives

In order to proactively set themselves on a steady and effective path toward the twenty-first century, the NPS introduced several

Opposite: Beautiful scenery continues to drive visitors to our national parks. Here, children walk along part of Utah's Arches National Park.

In the twenty-first century, parks are in the media spotlight (and in selfies!) more than ever before.

new initiatives between its seventy-fifth anniversary and the year 2000. There was the symposium in Vail, Colorado, that produced the Vail Agenda, a set of six recommendations that included education, access, leadership, professionalism, stewardship, science, and research. The agenda also pressed the NPS to partner at the state and local levels in order to better develop and manage the parks.

One key aspect of this partnering was a new initiative: national heritage areas (NHAs). These areas, which you may have seen designated through signage while driving through certain regions, are historic areas owned and managed by the state or local government that receive some grant funding and technical assistance from the NPS. There are currently forty-nine NHAs across the country, many of which stretch through multiple states. The Abraham Lincoln National Heritage Area in Illinois includes twenty sites, scattered throughout forty-two counties in the center of the state, and seeks to preserve and promote the heritage of the area in the context of Lincoln's life. The Mormon Pioneer National Heritage Area, located in Utah, spans a 400-mile (643 km) area and celebrates Utah's pioneer heritage, specifically that of Mormon pioneers. Several national parks and monuments lie within the larger area. Partnerships like these ensure that natural resources, recreational lands, and areas of historical significance aren't simply confined to spaces identified as national parks. Conservation and historic storytelling, which benefit the land and us, can happen both inside and outside park lines. In fact, if we prioritize initiatives like this one, they can happen almost anywhere.

The use of parks as a reminder of the United States' history was a central theme during the 1990s. New trails and battlefield memorials highlighting certain moments in history gave a voice to physical spaces while keeping valuable pieces of the nation's past in mind. During this period, the Selma to Montgomery National Historic Trail, located in Alabama, was created. It allowed visitors to trace the path of the 1965 marches for equal rights for African Americans. These protests, though intentionally nonviolent, were met by violence and brutality from law enforcement. Today, the historic trail provides a window into these events and a context in which to understand ongoing political and racial tensions in the United States today. Additionally, the Custer Battlefield National Monument was renamed the Little Bighorn Battlefield National Monument in 1991. This area memorializes a June battle between General George Armstrong Custer and the Seventh US Cavalry, and Lakota Sioux and Cheyenne warriors in 1876. This was one of the plains warriors' last armed attempts to preserve their way of life. By protecting and uplifting these areas as nationally recognized and valued symbols, with names upholding events rather than individuals involved, the NPS placed emphasis on reflection, history, culture, and community. These aspects would become some of their central goals in the twenty-first century.

While the lead-up to the millennium was busy with new parks, new partnerships, and goal-setting for the future, the NPS also had to worry about the day-to-day, the tedious business of keeping a large number of public areas up and running. One of the biggest concerns was ensuring more money was coming into the system. In 1995, the NPS increased fees for certain facilities and activities through a program called the Recreational Fee Demonstration Program. It allowed participating parks to retain the majority of revenues generated by their fees, though a small percentage of the revenue went to NPS initiatives and other

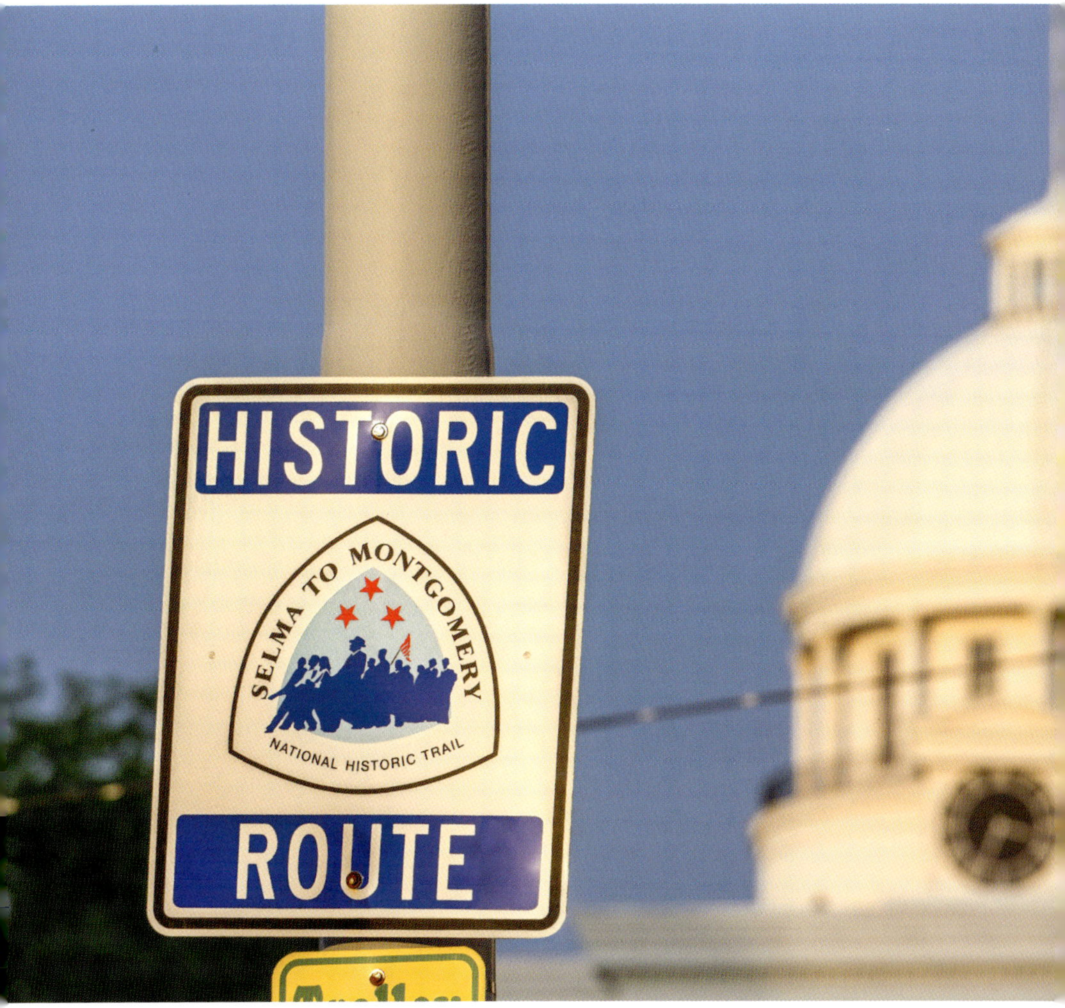

Signs like this one along the Selma to Montgomery National Historic Trail serve as markers for travelers who want to experience history right where it happened.

nonparticipating parks. Though it was simply a test, the program was extremely successful, so much so that in 2004, Congress voted to extend it through 2014. Today, when you pay a few dollars to enter a park or take part in certain activities within the parks, your money is being used for upkeep, preservation, and much more.

A Revised Mission for Changing Times

For the NPS, the year 2000 meant taking a hard look at their old mission statement and creating a revised version to reflect the changing times. The updated mission reused nearly all of the old language, but it also advanced several ideas to mission priorities: outdoor recreation, education, and inspiration. Though the enjoyment of nature within the parks has always been a key aspect, the NPS felt it was time to validate outdoor recreation, which hundreds of thousands of people participate in within the national parks each year. Skiing, hiking, canoeing, fishing, and so much more take place within the parks. Perhaps more so than simply sitting and staring at the beauty, or examining the natural resources for scientific research, physical interaction with the land has become a central focus for the parks and for the people who spend their free time there. The NPS also put the spotlight on education and inspiration of future generations, goals that, though always implicit for the NPS, were now explicitly stated and embraced. In order to protect the landscapes, stay relevant, and ensure the existence of the parks (and the planet) in the future, the NPS knew it needed to refocus its efforts on educating young people and providing them with new, inspirational connections to the parks.

The NPS's refocusing for the twenty-first century didn't end with its newly revised mission. In late 1999, the director of the NPS reached out to the National Park System Advisory Board, a committee of twelve individuals tasked with advising the director on matters relating to the NPS, and asked them to develop a report on the purposes and goals of the NPS for the next twenty-five years. In 2001, after consulting with academics, organizations, employees, and more, the board released its findings. "Rethinking the National Parks for the Twenty-First Century" lays out, in detail, the NPS's plan for the next several decades. In the report, they laid out several specific recommendations for changes, focuses, and advancements. Since the release of that report, the NPS has utilized it as a pathway for growth and development, as well as a tool for reflection about how far it has come in these first seventeen years of a new century.

Education and Learning

The national parks, with their **biodiversity**, magnificent landscapes, and rich histories, are some of the best classrooms in which to learn and grow. One cannot ignore the difference between reading about a salamander in a textbook and watching a salamander in its natural swamp habitat. Learning about the Grand Canyon and taking a hike in the Grand Canyon, feeling the heat on your neck and hearing your boots crunch against the ground, are two very different experiences. Experiential learning is the kind that sticks in one's mind and heart for a long time. It helps a person not only absorb and remember information but develop a connection to that information. It helps to answer the questions "Why do we have to learn this?" and "Why does this matter?"

While the NPS has always noted education as a part of its mission, it has only recently, in the last quarter-century or so, championed education as a defined, key portion that cannot be ignored and must not be avoided. In order to bring valuable information and experiences to America's changing population, the NPS has been working to diversify its education initiatives, developing programs, exhibits, and audiovisual presentations in multiple languages and for various ages. It now has programs catering to teenagers, including residential experiences, as well as programs that encourage families to engage with nature together. It has also brought technology into focus, especially in regards to distance learning. Through the internet, anyone can now engage with and share in the excitement of the parks. Slowly but surely, the NPS is embracing the internet in a more systematic way, even using social media to interact with the public and reinforce its presence in daily life.

Here is what the National Park System Advisory Board has to say about the education happening in the parks today:

> At Great Smoky Mountains National Park, high school and university students are helping catalogue species, an exercise that not only provides a much-needed inventory but also points the way into careers in biology. (A live moth trap devised by students has resulted in discovery of many new species of moths.) And in Lowell, Massachusetts, the Tsongas Industrial History Center represents a partnership between the Lowell National Historical Park and University of Massachusetts Lowell Graduate School of Education. At the Center, students can explore how canals advanced industrial expansion in the nineteenth century and

reenact, through role-playing episodes, the experiences of immigrant factory workers.

These are just a few examples of the ways in which the NPS has been working to expand education and increase its impact on youth and young adults in the twenty-first century.

Human and Environmental History

In discussions of history, it can be very easy to separate the history of humans—the structures built, the injustices enacted on one another, the things invented, etc.—and the history of the environment, the land, water, plants, and animals that are affected by human activity. In truth, these are seamlessly connected. The choices we make and have made historically change the way the environment lives, breathes, grows, and shrinks. Human actions change how landscapes look and feel. These actions, especially in the last couple hundred years, have impacted Earth and the atmosphere in a detrimental way. Today, extreme changes in climate are being experienced, as well as changes in glaciers, sea levels, and animal populations. While the NPS has always been tasked with preserving natural spaces, in the twenty-first century it has taken on the additional goal of preserving important places and relating broad historical-environmental themes to park visitors in order to ensure that the connection between human and environmental history is understood. This means not simply explaining that the glaciers are melting, but digging deeper into what specific human actions are causing Earth to warm, therefore melting the glaciers and making the sea levels rise.

By law, the National Park Service is charged with assisting in historic preservation on all federal lands, tribal reservations, and in the public and private sectors. It administers the National Historic Landmarks program and the National Register of Historic Places. The NPS also provides grants and tax incentives that encourage preservation of historic places. In so doing, the NPS hopes to reverse or slow some of the neglect that has come to historic sites and structures in recent years. Vandalism, inadequate funding, insensitive governmental policies, acid rain, and encroaching development all threaten historic sites. By maintaining historical structures, the NPS encourages the study of the American past and public exploration and discussion of that past. In this way, the NPS is doing its part to ensure that our future, especially as it relates to the environment, has a contextualized roadmap, a place from which to move forward, confident that we won't make the same mistakes again.

fact!

The National Historic Landmarks distinction belongs to over 2,500 historic places. The National Register of Historic Places has about 80,000 individual listings and millions of properties that are considered "contributing resources" within historic districts.

Conservation and Sustainability

Throughout the hundred-year history of the National Park Service, many complaints have been lodged against the NPS for its lack of science-based resource management. Science and scientific research has, for a long time, taken a "back seat" to beauty, recreation, and other aspects of the parks. For decades, there were no inventories of what currently exists in the parks in terms of wildlife. There were no action plans for dealing with the pressures of climate change. Both marine areas and parklands were seen as so vast, so far-reaching, that they wouldn't be affected by human activity. However, today, in the midst of the twenty-first century, the NPS sees clearly the need for dedication to conservation and resource management. Conservation, in this particular context, is the act of preserving, protecting, or restoring the natural environment. This can include natural ecosystems, vegetation, wildlife, marine areas, and more.

In order to conserve and manage its resources, the NPS is working to encourage **native species** and discourage non-native plants and animals. Native species originate in the areas where they are found. Be they plants or animals, non-native and invasive species can negatively impact ecosystems by disrupting the present food chains, forcing out native species, and even taking down whole swaths of forest or types of fish. Habitats are delicate things; the introduction of a non-native species or the disappearance of a regular, native species can have a huge impact on an ecosystem. Over the past 102 years, the NPS has learned that vegetation and wildlife are dynamic, not static. Plant and animal numbers are always in flux, and this requires that the NPS take an active role in monitoring them in order to ensure they are adequately protected. This work has already begun in earnest, with BioBlitzes (events that center around finding and identifying as many species as possible in a specific area in a short period of time) and other events encouraging the public to get involved in the counting of organisms within the parks. These inventories are now being accelerated in order to determine what appropriate actions, if any, need to be taken. The NPS is

Mount Rushmore National Memorial, located in the Black Hills of South Dakota, is just one example of the ways in which human history and environmental history cross paths and interact.

working to make conservation of biodiversity a core purpose of park management. It still has a long way to go.

In addition to its landholdings, the National Park Service oversees a significant number of shorelines, watersheds, marine sanctuaries, and other marine areas. These places, too, are threatened and in need of greater conservation. Pollutants, overfishing, shoreline development, and more are threatening the biodiversity of both freshwater and marine systems controlled by the NPS. Recently, the NPS has been working to alert the public to the overexploitation of these areas. This is an especially challenging venture, as marine life and water, in general, are often regarded as so vast as to not need human intervention. But fish species and marine plants are disappearing, and water quality declining. In order to slow or reverse the effects everyday human decisions are having on both lands and marine areas, the NPS has committed to stepping out in support of biodiversity and conservation in the twenty-first century.

One way the NPS has stepped up to ensure that environmental conservation remains central to its mission is through the Natural Resource Challenge. This program, created by Congress in 1999 at the request of the NPS, is a multiyear effort. It was initiated with the intention to double science efforts in national parks. It has not only doubled the NPS's natural resource budget from around $100 million per year to $200 million per year, but it includes many other strategies designed to improve knowledge of natural resources across the National Park System. It addresses three main challenges: to protect native species and their habitats, to provide leadership for a healthy environment, and to connect parks to both protected areas and to people. So far, the increased funding has introduced and expanded research, increased the

Threats to the environment are found in all of the national parks, including the Everglades in Florida, pictured here.

number and extent of recreation projects, improved education efforts, and increased the professional expertise of those who manage natural resources within the parks.

The NPS is also taking a stand for the environment in other ways—these days, it is working to make **sustainability** integral to its operations. While conservation is about the long-term, careful examination of species and ecosystems, sustainability deals with the day-to-day and how they carry out daily work with an eye to how environmental factors might affect the future. Facility management, waste disposal, recycling, and energy consumption are all important aspects of sustainability, and the National Park Service has examined each of these facets in recent years, especially as climate change and other pressures threaten the world. The NPS has stated that it recognizes the reality of climate change and the necessity of reducing energy consumption. In response to the changes, the NPS is employing scientists to conduct and apply research, it is working to reduce the **carbon footprint** of the NPS and the parks, and it is working to educate the public about climate change and sustainability efforts.

Recreation

More so today than ever before, the National Park Service believes that outdoor recreation is essential to the mental and physical health of all individuals. Fresh air, nature, new experiences, and the like have always been standout benefits of national parks, but with the advent of technology, increased development, and the allure of air-conditioned, comfortable indoor spaces, it is so much easier to choose staying indoors over adventuring. For decades, the US government has taken an active role in protecting and promoting outdoor recreation for Americans. The Outdoor Recreation Act, signed by President John F. Kennedy in May 1963, called on the federal government to promote the development of outdoor recreation programs. Additionally, legislation such as the National Trails System Act and the Urban Park and Recreation Recovery Act have promoted and expanded options for outdoor recreation, especially for those people living in urban areas, far from many of the expansive national parks.

Since 1981, when the NPS took over the Heritage Conservation and Recreation Service, the agency has more actively partnered with other organizations to create opportunities for recreation at the state and local levels. Through this initiative, the NPS has worked with communities to restore rivers, preserve open spaces, and develop trail networks. The NPS has also continued to provide grants toward the creation of baseball fields, biking paths, playgrounds, and other outdoor spaces for invaluable community recreation. Since they are often closer to home than national parks, these spaces create opportunities for more people to have outdoor recreation experiences, benefiting them in numerous ways. As the century progresses, the National Park Service will continue prioritizing and expanding recreation in the lives of all Americans, no matter how close they live to a national park.

People in Parks

In the lead-up to 2016, as part of its one hundredth birthday celebration, the National Park Service piloted several new initiatives aimed at getting people to the parks and celebrating their own personal connections to the parks and to the outdoors in general. In order to accomplish its goals of conservation, resource management, sustainability, history, education, and more, the NPS first had to capture the imaginations—and the time—of the American people. It had to get people to the parks, get them talking about the parks, cause them to remember positive experiences with the parks, and, in general, get them to "buy in" to the national parks and all they had to offer. This was a lofty goal, but the NPS tackled it on multiple fronts.

Perhaps the most recognizable initiative of the last couple years has been the Find Your Park campaign. This effort, coordinated jointly by the National Park Service and the National Park Foundation, as well as private partners like Disney, REI, American Express, and Subaru, aims to encourage people to find their personal connections to the national parks. Through a carefully planned, interactive website that makes generous use of visual media like photos and videos, the initiative is pushing to go viral, even creating its own hashtag for social media: #findyourpark. On the website (http://www.findyourpark.com), users can explore "stories," including videos and high-resolution photos of parks. While there, they can also make use of a comprehensive search feature that allows guests to limit results by state or activity. Those searching for geocaching, fly fishing, or whitewater rafting

fact!

In 2015, the National Park Service and the Girl Scouts announced a new partnership: the Girl Scout Ranger Program! This joint venture connects girls with NPS sites across the United States. The Boy Scouts have a history of similar partnerships with the NPS.

can quickly and easily find the right park here. Of course, those who want to swim or hike can certainly find a park, too. This online resource is making it simpler for families and individuals of all ages to see which park resources are available to them, and hopefully make use of them!

In addition to providing a searchable park database, the NPS has also been working, again in collaboration with the National Park Foundation, to spearhead an initiative focused on connecting more kids to national parks through fun and engaging activities. This project, called Open Outdoors for Kids, is guided by research that tells us that children who spend time outdoors are healthier and do better in school. The program helps them to be more proficient in science and have a more comprehensive understanding of history. It also acknowledges that cutbacks in school funding have created barriers to accessing the outdoors, especially for children from underserved, urban communities.

Open Outdoors for Kids addresses these barriers in several ways. Through a program called Ticket to Ride, it provides educators and children with transportation, programs, and free entry to the parks so that they can participate in immersive educational experiences. It connects kids and families to the parks through National Park Foundation grants for cultural programs and restoration activities. And it establishes opportunities and sites for education within the parks, creating opportunities for children, families, and teachers to engage with each other in the great outdoors.

What's Next?

The twenty-first century has, so far, presented both challenges and exciting opportunities for the National Park Service and

Women in the NPS

Throughout the history of the National Park Service, gender equality has been a sticky issue, but in the twenty-first century, the workforce has become slightly more balanced. There were very few female rangers during the first years of the NPS, but as the years went on, women gained entry into the organization through clerical work. In the 1960s and 1970s, visitors began to see more women in the ranger uniform and even some in positions of leadership.

The NPS has been slow to change. Women couldn't wear the traditional NPS uniform until 1978! Since that time, there have been many female superintendents and regional directors, though only two women have been appointed to the top director position. Issues with gender and diversity are still present in the NPS. Following its one hundredth year of operations, women still make up less than half of the NPS workforce.

Members of the Northwest Youth Corps work on a trail at Mount Rainier National Park in July 2016.

its partners. A changing climate, continued development, and other environmental challenges have turned up the pressure both inside the parks and across the globe, necessitating the NPS's response. Efforts toward effective historic preservation, increased recreation, and expanded education initiatives have all helped to keep the NPS on the map as an effective, dynamic, relevant, forward-thinking agency that has a pulse on what the nation needs. As the NPS works its way through funding changes, a tense political landscape, and continued environmental pressures, it remains to be seen how it will respond and change in order to meet those challenges. It is clear, however, that the NPS hopes to continue its current trajectory of focused, sustainable goals and actions, and that it will continue to figure out how it can serve *all* American people, as well as *all* natural resources, as best as it can.

Driving Along

When you think of the national parks, you probably picture mountains, trees, trails … and roads? Maybe not. But certain roads are a big part of the NPS, the parks themselves, and the visitor experience. In the 1910s and 1920s, the National Park-to-Park Highway, an auto trail, was constructed in order to loop together twelve national parks in the West. The highway connects Yellowstone, Glacier, Mount Rainier, Yosemite, Sequoia, Zion, Grand Canyon, and more.

The highway, though today a smooth and well-known route, was a bold move for the turn of the century. However, following World War I, as automobiles became accessible and popular with more Americans, auto trails began to take off, and the Park-to-Park Highway became a favorite trip for families. The scenic drive extends for about 5,600 miles (8,529 km) and travels through eleven states.

SMOKEY
FIRE DANGER
HIGH
TODAY!
SMOKEY
PREVENT FOREST FIRES

3

The NPS and Society

It is easy to tell the story of how American society has both positively and negatively influenced the National Park Service. With its mission and goals of protecting and conserving treasured natural resources, the NPS directly serves citizens of the past, present, and future. It honors moments and movements in US history and makes sure that people of all ages have beautiful places to enjoy. These are things that citizens desire and request. Over one hundred years ago, a coordinated push from explorers, artists, politicians, conservationists, and others resulted in the creation of the NPS. Today, it is the American people who keep the NPS going. With visits, tax dollars, votes, and passion for the outdoors, people make sure the parks stay open and accessible to all who wish to enjoy them.

On the other hand, it is a bit more complicated, though no less inspiring, to discuss the ways in which the National Park Service

Opposite: Smokey the Bear, a national icon since 1944, is used to warn park visitors of fire risks.

has influenced society. It has had economic impact, churning billions of dollars through local, state, and national economies. It has had environmental impact, protecting countless species within the parks and spreading the word about climate change. Moreover, it has had cultural impact, lifting up the idea of the public good, shared spaces, and the value of cultural conservation. In these ways and more, the NPS has expanded well beyond the early days of dusty stagecoach rides for the lucky few who could travel to enjoy the parks. Today, the NPS works hard to make sure that the parks are open and accessible to all. In this way, their influence is exponentially greater, and their impact is truly remarkable.

Economic Impact

National parks, monuments, and heritage areas are not often situated in heavily populated areas. Though there are some urban locations overseen by the NPS, most of the parks need room; as wild, natural areas, national parks are usually set apart from residential zones. However, this does not mean that lands held by the NPS are necessarily completely separate from towns, residences, and businesses. On the contrary, the national parks, on a whole, serve as economic engines for many local communities, and are powerful parts of economic vitality for many states and larger regions as well. Without the Grand Canyon, nearly five million visitors would probably be less inclined to make the trek out to Arizona each year, and the many hotels, restaurants, and other businesses that profit from tourists would be at a loss. Similarly, thousands of people who work in the tourist industry near the canyon, not to mention in the park itself, would need to find other work. Parks truly keep communities running. Their economic impact runs deep.

Millions of people visit the parks each year. Most of these are visitors from other parts of the United States or other parts of the world, which means they have to travel to reach the park. Once they arrive at the parks, visitors often stay for a night or more in order to make the most of their trip. They might spend money to camp at a locally owned campsite, then spend more money at the local grocery store to get hot dogs, s'mores, gasoline, or bug spray. A visit to a national park requires an amount of gear, even for a quick trip! In 2016, national park visitors spent $18.4 billion in local **gateway regions** while visiting NPS-managed lands across the country. The term "gateway community" refers to a city or town adjacent to a national park. A gateway to a park offers restaurants, shops, campgrounds, hotels, and places in which one can learn about the park's resources. The large number of visitors that a gateway region sees in a given year strongly influences the local economy, as well as the social fabric of an area. In 2016, the top national parks by visitor spending included Blue Ridge, Great Smoky Mountains, Grand Canyon, Denali, and Grand Teton National Parks. That means that their local regions were probably highly affected both economically and socially by visitors. Spending in and around the Blue Ridge Parkway nearly topped $1 billion in 2016! That money goes a long way when it comes to the development and continued vibrancy of a town or region.

fact!

In 2016, over 330 million people visited national parks over the course of the calendar year.

In addition to visitor spending at local businesses, it is important to remember that businesses spend money at other businesses. A restaurant might buy

Many national parks feature historic lodgings like this one, the Majestic Yosemite Hotel, which help keep local economies running.

vegetables from a local farmer. A hotel may get its uniforms cleaned by a local cleaning service. The park itself might even make use of local businesses and services for its daily operation. All of this spending couldn't happen without employment. Employees of the parks (twenty-two thousand across the country) use their income to purchase goods and services in the local economy. When park visitors spend money at local businesses, the owners and employees from those businesses use their own incomes to spend money in the region. This further amplifies the effect of visitor spending. In fact, it is estimated that the Grand Canyon helps to produce and maintain nearly ten thousand jobs in the region, bringing in over $300 million in labor income for regional workers in 2016.

On a national scale, the national parks contributed over 315,000 jobs to gateway regions in 2016, largely in the restaurant, hotel, and recreation sectors. Federal lands also serve to attract workers to them. People often choose to move, not only for jobs but for lifestyles. If living near a national park allows you to mountain bike, ski, or hike every single day—what's not to love? Lance Trebesche, CEO of TicketPrinting.com, says: "Our quality of life is defined by our public lands and access to them. This gives us and other tech companies in Montana a distinct competitive advantage. We can recruit and retain top talent successfully within and outside the state because of the world-class landscape that surrounds us." National parks don't simply create jobs, they help create communities of motivated, successful individuals who love where they live.

While many people move to gateway regions to find work within the national parks, as rangers or educators, or outside the national parks, in private businesses that benefit from being in close proximity to the park, others choose a third

fact!

The Commercial Services Program of the National Park Service issues about five hundred concession contracts each year, most of them to returning businesses.

option—they work for privately held companies that operate from inside national parks. These businesses are a special kind, called **concessioners**. A concessioner is a private business that has a contract with the federal government that allows them to operate inside the public parkland. Some of these are lodges, like Badlands Lodge, LLC, which operates within Badlands National Park, or Pisgah Inn, which operates in Blue Ridge. Others deal with recreation, like those that provide private boat rentals, trail rides, cycling, or seaplanes. Still other concessioners provide food, ferry services, gas stations, or even cruising, such as the cruise companies that dock in Alaskan national parklands. These concession contracts not only provide jobs for workers and businesses in which to spend money, but they are life-giving for the handful of companies who count on their contract with NPS to exist at all. In order for park visitors to be well rested, well fed, and capable of appreciating the national parks to their fullest extent, the NPS depends on concessioners. The NPS's history with private companies stretches all the way back to Yellowstone's designation in 1872.

The ripple effects caused by visitors, spending, employment, and labor income all result in large amounts of total economic output. In 2016, the national parks contributed nearly $35 billion to the national economy. Spread out among states and gateway regions, that is an incredible amount of money that has helped bolster living conditions and economic outlook for people from

Even in secluded park areas, today's visitors stay connected through various forms of technology—for better or worse.

California to Florida. From the Hawaiian volcanoes to the Alaskan wilderness, one cannot escape the economic impact that the national parks and the National Park Service have on gateway communities, local economies, state economies, and even the national economy.

Environmental Impact

In addition to funneling billions of dollars into the national, state, and local economies, the National Park Service has been, especially in recent years, a major driver of environmental initiatives and a fairly outspoken leader in the fight to recognize and slow the effects of climate change. In 2016, the NPS issued the "National Climate Change Interpretation and Education Strategy," outlining a strategy to engage visitors on climate change topics. Today, we live in a world in which climate change is not accepted as fact by all people or formal parties. The National Park Service, as a respected and well-known federal agency, has the unique ability to inspire public thought, discussion, and even action on all sorts of topics. About their motivation to create the strategy, the NPS says, "[Climate change] is an overarching and omnipresent influence on every acre under the care of the National Park Service (NPS). The changing climate surrounds us, compelling us to tell the story." Thankfully, the national parks also "surround" the American people, both literally and figuratively, so the messages communicated by the NPS have the power to reach many individuals and make a real impact on how Americans think and talk about climate change. The NPS is uniquely positioned to advance this dialogue.

The National Park Service has developed a climate change communications strategy based around three goals. The first, "Provide opportunities to find personal relevance in relation to climate change," is an especially important one. It is difficult to convince someone to believe in something they cannot necessarily touch and see. The parks, because they are tangible and experiential, are the perfect environments in which to engage people on climate issues. The effects are present, clear, and touchable. Things like melting glaciers, changing ecosystems, and frequent wildfires are hard to ignore, especially if you are standing right in front of them. When a park can act as a "natural laboratory" of sorts and connect people of all ages with the environment, the parks are making a difference in the climate change conversation.

The second goal of the strategy is to "develop a climate-conscious workforce." This means providing climate change resources and training to all staff and partners of the National Park Service. Interpreters, educators, and volunteers play a significant role in the experiences that park visitors have when they walk (or drive) through the park entrance gates. These trained, trustworthy individuals must be well equipped to engage with the public about climate change, because the everyday visitor cannot interpret for himself or herself the effects the climate is having on the park. A ranger can engage an individual about disappearing honeybees just by crouching down, pointing to a flower, and telling a story. Today, the NPS is dedicated to providing training, tools, and techniques for its in-park workers and volunteers, helping them provide consistent, clear communication about climate change.

The third goal as outlined in the NPS's strategy is to "provide leadership in national and global climate change response." As a trusted source of informal education, the NPS has the unique opportunity to engage audiences on the ways in which climate change is affecting the national parks, how humans may need to adapt in coming years, and what we can do now to shrink our carbon footprints. The NPS can model behaviors,

The NPS cultivates a culture of sustainability and biodiversity through partnerships with biologists like Mark Mendelsohn, shown here examining red-legged frog eggs in Upper Las Virgenes Canyon Open Space Preserve.

actions, and communications. They hope to continue promoting climate literacy and showcasing sustainable practices, especially local opportunities.

Lastly, the NPS hopes to "cultivate a community of climate communication with [their] partners," an effort that highlights the need for collaboration with local communities, other agencies and organizations, educational partners, volunteer networks, and more. This goal, if completed, will serve to amplify the messages of the NPS, getting the message out louder, and to many more people, that climate change is real and urgent and caused by human behavior. To this end, the NPS has made their resources extremely accessible, helped to build and strengthen support networks, cultivated partnerships at many levels, and used its own park sites to promote community discussion and engagement around climate change. Though none of these goals alone will successfully spread the news of climate change and what we can do about it, taken together they could help mitigate the effects we are already seeing.

Communication strategies are an extremely important part of the work the NPS is doing to combat climate change, but they aren't the only part. In 2010, the NPS created and published its official strategy to directly address the impacts of climate change. Its four components—science, mitigation, adaptation, and communication—are less about expressing the realities of climate change to visitors, educators, and partners, and more about *doing* something. Just as climate change threatens the world around us, it also directly threatens the national parks. In order to deal with those threats, the NPS is called to act.

One prong of the NPS strategy is science. Over the last ten years, and for as long as the strategy remains in place, the NPS will conduct scientific research and assessments, collaborate with scientific agencies and institutions, and learn from the best available climate change science, applying it to park management as it goes along. It is developing integrated data systems, using state-of-the-art technology, in order to efficiently discover and share climate change information. Planning, adapting, and monitoring are cornerstones of the NPS science-focused climate strategy. The NPS is also developing and applying an approach for reducing its carbon footprint and potential options for carbon storage and sequestration on NPS lands, though there are still many ecological consequences of sequestration to be considered. Carbon sequestration involves removing carbon dioxide from the atmosphere and holding it, in a solid or liquid form, often under the earth. It has been suggested as a way to slow the accumulation of greenhouse gases in the atmosphere, effectively deferring global warming. However, there are still many unknowns when it comes to the science and its effects, and the NPS isn't jumping on board just yet.

Another strategy put forth by the NPS to deal with climate change is adaptation. Adaptation refers to adjustments in systems in order to moderate harm. In order to make certain that cultural and natural resources, as well as infrastructure, will continue to exist within the national parks, the NPS must adapt, potentially affecting all NPS operations. The NPS has committed to incorporating climate change considerations and responses into all levels of planning going forward. This includes vulnerability assessments, conservation plans, inventories, and more.

Additionally, the National Park Service has made a commitment to mitigation. By limiting NPS greenhouse gas emissions and reducing the carbon footprint of NPS operations, the NPS can become a leader to park visitors, organizational partners, and communities. Energy and water conservation, alternative transportation, sustainable facility design and operation, behavior change, new technology, recycling, wastewater recovery, and so much more is woven into the NPS plan for mitigation. The fourth prong, communication, sets goals for the NPS to develop key messages about climate change that it can then share both inside and outside the parks.

In addition to the strategies outlined above, the National Park Service also has a Green Parks Plan for 2016 based on ten goals. These focus, for the most part, on the impact of facilities. The NPS has outlined a number of reachable goals and strategies that will hopefully help it to not only reduce its carbon footprint and mitigate the unwelcome effects of climate change, but also effectively harness its leadership and communication to spread messages to individuals, organizations, and communities across the country, multiplying the strength of its voice.

Cultural and Community Impact

Since its founding, the National Park Service has served not only as an environmental leader or economic driver. It has also impacted society on a cultural and community level, sharing its ideas, resources, and inspiration across the country and the world. Its community impact is immense. The NPS has a long history of programs and initiatives—outside of the well-known parks—that empower specific communities through historic preservation, environmental conservation, the creation of recreation areas, and so much more.

Many local parks and natural areas are not only inspired by the success of the national parks but are driven to acquire the resources and expertise that can help them complete park projects at home, though home might be far away from the nearest

Community-led restoration projects, like this tree-planting day hosted with community college students, do the dual job of educating and engaging visitors and restoring environments within national parks.

national park. The NPS employs a national network of planning professionals who partner with community groups, state and local governments, nonprofits, tribes, and others to create recreation opportunities, design trails and parks, protect special places, and so much more. The program that supports "community-led natural resource conservation and outdoor recreation projects across the nation" is called the Rivers, Trails, and Conservation Assistance Program. As the title says, they focus on rivers, trails, recreation, and conservation, and work with groups in urban, suburban, and rural areas. The application process is straightforward and accessible; over 350 communities participated in 2017!

In Philadelphia, Pennsylvania, the NPS has partnered with a community organization to complete the Mantua Greenway project, which will renovate a community greenway, adding trees, planning for storm water management, and installing public art. In Danville, Illinois, the NPS worked with Danville residents to develop a 2.5-mile (4 km) trail plan connecting downtown Danville to the Kickapoo Rail Trail. And in Seattle, Washington, as of 2017, the NPS is developing a park, in collaboration with sponsors and a partner group, that will include wetland restoration, STEM education, and a food garden. Area residents and students are involved in the planning, hands-on monitoring, restoration, and design. Projects like these are just a few shining examples of the impactful work being done by the Rivers, Trails, and Conservation Assistance Program. Through this program, the NPS works to help communities empower themselves to take parks and conservation into their own hands and turn their dreams into reality.

Since the very beginning of the National Park Service, art and visual media have played an important role. Before the NPS was created, artists traveled to Yellowstone to sketch it, sending pictures to newspapers to prove its existence and majesty. When it came time to form the NPS, it was the artists and writers who convinced the public and policymakers that the beauty of the parks was worth protecting with federal designation. Today, that legacy continues. The NPS manages an artist-in-residence program that allows visual artists, writers, musicians, and other creators to live in one of the parks for two to four weeks. Oftentimes, artists are required to participate in park programs and share their creations with the public. In addition to residencies officially offered by the NPS, the agency also allows other nonprofit organizations to run their own residencies within the parks. All of this activity amounts to parks that, during a good portion of the year, are filled with people making all sorts of art, from dance to paintings to poems.

The NPS also has several programs in place that commemorate specific times and places in history, such as Native American graves, Japanese American confinement sites, and battlefields. In 1990, the NPS was directed to begin a special resource study on alternatives for commemorating and interpreting the Underground Railroad. The study, which involved special consultation with community advocates and local researchers, was completed in 1995. At that time, the NPS formally established the National Underground Railroad Network to Freedom, a program that preserves sites associated with the Underground Railroad, educates the public, and promotes programs and partnerships. Today, the program hosts an annual conference, bringing together researchers, scholars, advocates, site stewards, and government officials to explore history together. It also has an online database and many curriculum-based lesson plans in addition to the network of historic sites associated with the Underground Railroad. Together, the pieces of the Underground

Railroad Network to Freedom, including the programs, sites, and education efforts, all form a mosaic of stories that help to educate those who come into contact with the network and its components.

Historically, urban communities, and especially minority communities, have had limited access to the national parks. In fact, outdoor recreation in general has often been available only to those who have the time, money, and other privileges that allow them to seek it out and feel comfortable within park settings. For a few decades, however, urban neighborhoods were able to benefit from the Urban Park and Recreation Recovery Program (UPARR), authorized in 1978. This program gave matching grants to economically distressed urban communities in order to revitalize and improve recreation opportunities. In 1978, the National Urban Recreation Study, done by the Department of the Interior, concluded that urban park and recreation facilities were deteriorating and needed federal funds in order to restore them. The resulting legislation gave local governments and counties the opportunity to apply for matching funds. Over the years, rehabilitation has been completed on playgrounds, recreation centers, swimming pools, basketball courts, and community centers. UPARR also provided "innovation" grants that covered the costs of providing or augmenting recreation services at the neighborhood level, as well as grants to develop park and recreation plans. The program encouraged local planning and a commitment to continued operation and maintenance of programs and facilities. Unfortunately, the program has gone unfunded since 2002. Its legacy is now marked more by its current lack of funding and the continued lack of support for under-resourced, economically disadvantaged urban neighborhoods than it is by the hundreds of projects completed during its active years.

Sites like the Mayhew Cabin in Nebraska, pictured here with the sign John Brown's Cave, are noted on the NPS's National Underground Railroad Network to Freedom program.

In countless ways over the past 102 years, the National Park Service has reflected and impacted American society, and its influence can still be seen today. Whether it is adding jobs and wealth to local, state, and national economies; educating the public about the importance of mitigating climate change; or helping local communities improve the trail systems in their own backyards, the NPS is constantly at work in the lives of Americans all across the country.

National Parks vs. National Forests

Public land designations can be extremely confusing. Preserves, areas, parks, forests, recreation areas, sites—what's the difference? Some regions even fall into multiple categories and have more than one designation. When it comes to distinguishing between a national forest and a national park, it's helpful to remember that the NPS as an organization was a "spin-off" of the US Forest Service, though the first national park was created years before the first national forest. Yellowstone was established as the first national park in 1872. The Forest Reserve Act didn't come along until 1891, allowing the president to establish forest reserves. In 1905, the forests were transferred from the Department of the Interior to the Department of Agriculture. The US Forest Service was created that year. The NPS was created in 1916.

Aside from being managed under different departments, the greatest difference between national forests and national parks is their mandated use. Parks are to be preserved and changed very little. As physical spaces, they are rarely altered. Forests, on the other hand, are cut for timber and used for recreation, grazing, wildlife, and more. They are to be put to productive use, rather than preserved for their natural and cultural resources. One might also note that the US Forest Service is over two times the size of the National Park System. It includes 193 million acres (78,104,328 ha), 155 national forests, 20 national grasslands, and 1 national tallgrass prairie.

4

Challenges Faced Then and Now

From its earliest days, the national parks have not been without threats to their existence, their resources, and their accessibility to all people across America. Simply getting federal designation for the parks was a struggle in itself, and the creation of the National Park Service required many participants to give impassioned pleas. Since then, the NPS has stayed afloat through two world wars, the Great Depression, and countless other military conflicts across the globe, not to mention natural disasters and fluctuating budgets due to an ever-changing political landscape. The NPS has endured controversy and complaints. However, today it is up against some of the biggest challenges it has ever faced, and possibly the most immense challenges it will face in our lifetime. Environmental pressures, including global warming, are bearing down on the planet and its natural spaces. Additionally, today's environment is a particularly tough one for

Opposite: As the NPS winds its way into this next century, it is engaging everyone—even children and families—in environmental work and "citizen science" efforts.

public funding, and many parks have started to rely on public-private partnerships and foundations to secure the funds they need to keep the parks running. In these changing times, parks are also struggling with the invasion of technology within their natural borders. Those in leadership positions, as well as rangers on the ground, are forced to reckon with the pervasiveness of smartphones, data, etc., and are slowly but surely developing plans that will help them navigate this tech-savvy world in the coming years. Taken together, these challenges may seem insurmountable, but the NPS has a long history of overcoming obstacles. It is committed to staying true to its mission no matter what.

Threats to the Environment

External threats to the parks were first intentionally documented in 1980 in the NPS's State of the Parks Report. This report detailed the first NPS-wide survey that was conducted in order to identify threats to the parks' natural and cultural resources. Specifically, the report to Congress outlined pollutants, visitor activities, invasive species, and development, among other factors that were threatening the parks. Since that report, the threats have only grown worse, and solutions are not quickly at hand.

External forces continue to put pressure on the parks. Some of this comes from the outside—from continued development that slowly encroaches on parklands. We are long past the days of remote parks that took days to reach. Today, many national parks are a short drive from major cities, which have begun to expand, planting gas stations, shopping centers, and housing developments closer to park borders. Parking lots spread far and wide. Even industries are expanding, pushing the limit on just how close to a park a company can get when mining, logging, extracting natural gas, and more. All of this development seems innocuous at first, since it can bring more visitors and industry to help support a park region, but it has had adverse effects on wildlife. For instance, it has disrupted migration areas for birds, fish, and other species that rely on natural migration patterns. "Bird traffic" gets more and more interrupted, too. Human–wildlife conflicts are also occurring more frequently, as animals like wolves, bears, and bison accidentally cross park boundaries and find themselves face-to-face with humans.

As more land around the parks is developed, the NPS is also seeing higher rates of air and water pollution. Vehicle emissions from cars driving into and near the parks, industrial waste, and power-plant emissions are all clouding the air in the parks. Particulates—microscopic solid or liquid matter—are poisonous to plants and animals. Additionally, high mercury levels have been found in many species in Mammoth Cave National Park, Big Bend National Park, the Everglades, Acadia, and more. Mercury in fish, birds, and bats not only threatens the health of those species, but of any predator (including humans!) that eats those animals. Mercury can also negatively affect reproduction and foraging. Today, other than the slow but continuous closure of coal-fired power plants that we've seen over the last few years (but which isn't guaranteed to last), there is no long-term, large-scale plan in place to combat water and air pollution within the national parks.

fact!

In 128 national parks, air-pollution levels regularly exceed national standards.

The same residential and commercial development that is creeping around park borders is also bringing with it new

Nowadays, cars and campers cause noise and air pollution in the United States' most natural, protected spaces.

advances in energy production. Unfortunately, humans are always consuming more energy, which means production and mining must be continuous. Thousands of mining claims are currently being considered just outside the borders of national parks. Near Theodore Roosevelt National Park in the Badlands, oil and gas wells have been multiplying within the region, causing both air pollution and light pollution, as well as strong odors and noise. The creation of new uranium mines near the Grand Canyon had been temporarily banned in 2012, but in 2017, the possibility of resuming the expansion of operations there threatened wildlife and water resources. Similarly, plans to build a hydroelectric plant near Eagle Mountain, California, were seen as a possible threat to the desert ecosystem of nearby Joshua Tree National Park. Several national parks in Alaska were also eyed as regions fit for open-pit copper and gold mines. All of these mining operations could be threats to the natural environments located within the national parks' borders. Most of the initiatives were negotiated and opposed by visitors, employees, and activists who wanted to see the parks unaltered by pollution. Writing letters, making phone calls, and telling stories about the parks can go a long way to stave off drilling and mining, but they aren't always successful. It would take continued and increased effort and coordination to protect such park borderlands in the coming years.

Though development, industries, energy production, and other forms of physical human creations are harming the parks in a real way, there is one challenge that is so big, so far-reaching, and so tough to grasp that the pressure on the NPS is truly unrelenting. Climate change is affecting each and every one of the national parks, and will continue to do so for the foreseeable future. Most of us have heard about the melting glaciers at Glacier,

Olympic, and Mount Rainier National Parks, which are expected to be gone by 2030, but shifting precipitation patterns, rising temperatures, droughts, coastal erosion, storms, wildfires, and more threaten all of the parks. These effects of climate change threaten all types of park resources, not just natural—historical, cultural, and practical resources like restrooms and roads could also be harmed and changed. Perhaps the most frustrating and difficult part of climate change is that it creates uncertainty; even though we know Earth is warming, we cannot perfectly predict the weather emergencies, extreme temperatures, and more that can (and will) result from that warmth.

Today, the NPS is doing several things to mitigate the negative effects of climate change. It is working to restore ecosystems and prepare them for an ever-warming future, gathering information to increase biodiversity within its parks. Though these plans are currently in place, and have been for many years now, we cannot expect the NPS alone to "solve" climate change issues within its parks. This is a global problem that needs people and systems to make very big sacrifices and changes if we are going to mitigate the situation whatsoever. In order to help the public get a better understanding of the effects and threats of climate change, the NPS is making an intentional, focused effort to educate park visitors about climate change through daily conversations with visitors, official statements and reports, and strategic partnerships. People young and old need to know the ways in which humans are contributing to global warming and what that means for our planet.

Technology

While there have been many books written on environmental threats to the parks and what to do about them, another challenge

The effects of climate change can be seen all across our planet, especially in the retreating glaciers, like this one located (for now) in the Canadian Rockies.

This postcard from around 1960 shows the entrance to Yellowstone, decades before the advent of Wi-Fi and social media.

lurks within the home, and probably within the backpack or pocket of nearly every person who visits the parks during a typical year. As smartphones, tablets, drones, and other mobile technologies become more and more widespread, the NPS is working to adapt and thinking about how it will address the slew of issues that technology brings when it travels into rustic, natural environments.

There have always been debates about how wired the parks should be. Some feel that digital dependence has reached such a high level within the US that all of the national parks should have Wi-Fi access, charging stations, and other conveniences for our ever-connected culture. Without a connected and charged device, visitors cannot easily use GPS, quickly access park information online, share photos of their experiences in real time, or even check the weather! The NPS is considering offering Wi-Fi at some parks, but only in buildings and developed areas—not at the bottom of the Grand Canyon or deep in the Shenandoah woods. In fact, the Grand Canyon is currently piloting a program that allows visitors to access ranger narration along the South Rim. These short pieces offer comments about air quality, plants, animals, geology, and Native American history. Still, critics argue that any disruption of the parks' pristine peace and solitude is a negative one.

The NPS, for its part, wants to stay relevant. This isn't the first time it's dived into difficult conversations surrounding new advancements. At one time, cars, electric lights, and swimming pools were all questionable park additions. Today, one can hardly picture the national parks without these things! Currently, the NPS is looking into ways in which digital tools can be embraced in order to attract and retain young visitors. Twitter users can get updates from Old Faithful by following the handle @GeyserNPS, and the NPS's new #FindYourPark campaign actively promotes real-time photo-sharing on Instagram and other platforms, all from within the national parks. At Alaska's Katmai National Park, you can stand on a platform and watch bears catch salmon out of the Brooks River or walk through the forest. You can also turn to Katmai's bear cameras, which broadcast live footage of the bears, both on land and underwater. If marine life is more your style, you can watch sea lions, fish, and anemones go about their daily lives through the Channel Islands National Park's "Kelp Cam."

In some locations, the NPS is actually harnessing the innovative, technology-savvy minds of the youth in order to understand the ways in which tech can play a positive, nonintrusive role within the parks. At Acadia National Park in Maine, the park has started a teen-led group called the Acadia Youth Technology Team, tasked with figuring out how to use technology within Acadia. Some of their projects have included installing their own wildlife cam in a falcon nest, labeling plants with **QR codes** so visitors can look up additional information, and making a 3D model of a walrus skull.

For now, technology in the parks remains controversial, and the issue will probably demand compromise from all sides. We cannot slow or stop the future, especially when it comes to technological advancements.

Funding and Government

In order to continue on its current trajectory of mitigating climate change and environmental threats as much as it possibly can and continuing to educate both children and adults (even if it means dealing with short attention spans and distracting smartphones),

A park ranger working at Grand Teton National Park teaches children about the park while on a hike through the forest.

fact!

As of 2017, many national parks cannot hire the workers they need due to budget cuts. The Blue Ridge Parkway has had seventy-five vacant positions since 2003, which they are unable to fill until more funding arrives.

the NPS is in constant need of funding. Since its inception, the NPS has only grown, adding parks, monuments, programs, educational opportunities, and other initiatives that cost money, all on top of everyday maintenance and upkeep of the core parks. Across the country, the national parks have had to scrimp for more than a decade, deferring maintenance and construction projects as they limp along. According to the *Washington Post*, the Blue Ridge Parkway (a road/park system that curves through the Appalachian Mountains for 469 miles (755 km) has a $385 million backlog of projects. Of great concern, in the case of the Blue Ridge, are road projects that can affect safety for drivers.

Lack of funding isn't a new issue for the NPS. In fact, federal funding has always provided only a portion of the funds needed for most major national parks to run effectively. Many of the parks have **friends groups**, supportive organizations that raise private funds for particular parks and projects. The NPS even has its own congressionally chartered organization, the National Park Foundation (NPF). Each year, the NPF and the friends groups raise critical funds needed to keep the parks operating at their full potential. The Yellowstone Park Foundation, formed in 1996, has raised over $85 million and funded more than three hundred important projects that the federal government simply cannot cover. The foundation supports wildlife research, youth education,

Tweeting from the National Parks ... Or Not

In early 2017, the US Department of the Interior came under fire from the newly inaugurated president, Donald Trump, after the National Park Service retweeted a post that compared the size of the crowd at the president's inauguration to the larger crowd at President Obama's 2009 ceremony. They also retweeted a statement that referenced the removal of climate change language from the White House website. Immediately following the posts, the NPS social media team was ordered to halt operations and shut down the Twitter accounts.

Following the enforced shutdown of the NPS Twitter account, as well as the social media blackout of the Environmental Protection Agency, the Badlands National Park Twitter account took matters into its own hands, posting several facts about climate change on its official Twitter account. Soon, other alternative NPS accounts joined in the resistance, posting facts about the issues.

While the NPS has a complicated history with technology, it is currently serving to help social media at some parks, and sometimes whole organizations, proclaim exactly where they stand on important issues, letting their voices be heard even in times when their freedom of speech could be restricted if they say the "wrong" thing.

trail restoration, and other initiatives that lie just outside of basic park operation.

At Grand Teton National Park in northwestern Wyoming, the ragged skyline, formed perhaps ten million years ago, reminds visitors of Earth's extreme age. The park, encompassing over 310,000 acres (125,452 ha), hosts four million visitors each year. It has the nation's most comprehensive Native American art and artifact collections, representing over one hundred tribes. It also includes old dude ranches, a ferry, cabins, and rock walls for recreation. The Grand Tetons are cherished by millions, but limited federal funding has resulted in a maintenance backlog and put a strain on park services. Much-loved areas within the park, like beautiful Jenny Lake, are in sharp decline. Fortunately, the Grand Teton National Park Foundation exists, and it steps up each year to help in a huge way. The NPF has helped make improvements in education and outreach, providing a $25 million state-of-the-art facility, the Craig Thomas Discovery and Visitor Center, in 2007. In addition to youth outreach and education, the NPF avidly supports wildlife research and protection. Without the NPF, Grand Teton National Park would look and feel like a different park. Until the federal government steps up and commits to funding US national parks, private philanthropy will be a necessary component of national parks in the twenty-first century.

Private-Public Partnerships

One option for national parks in need of funding is to rely more heavily on private-public partnerships. In these relationships, the National Park Service still owns the land and regulates the area, but a private company (or even a private entrepreneur, an individual) runs the day-to-day operations of the park. In this model, the goal of the park is to generate a profit for the manager. In Arizona, most of the state parks are run by a private company called Recreation Resource Management. While this isn't necessarily the best model for every park—some worry that it could lead to exploitation of the land, or turn the parks into amusement-park-style attractions—under economic pressure, park managers will have to find a way to make ends meet, and public-private partnerships could be one small step toward a healthy solution.

5

The Legacy of the NPS

On August 25, 2016, the National Park Service turned one hundred years old. Over the course of the century, the NPS has grown from a fledgling organization with no funding and few visitors to a system that covers more than 84 million acres (33.9 million ha) across the United States. With over four hundred sites, the NPS has something for everyone. As forms of public good, the parks are meant to be shared and enjoyed by anyone who might want to see their sights, hike their trails, or make use of their recreation areas. From the reverent, flat skyline of Antietam National Battlefield in Maryland to the loud, proud majesty of Arches National Park in Utah, the NPS oversees a diverse array of sites. It has some of America's "best-kept secrets" and many well-loved, popular spots to visit. However, the NPS is more than just a system of pretty places.

Opposite: The view from above Calcite Springs offers one of the best lookouts in Yellowstone National Park.

In its mission, the NPS is called to preserve park resources for future generations. Today, heavy emphasis has been placed on education and scientific research, both of which serve to uphold the mission of preservation while acknowledging the importance of "future generations." These two components help form the lasting legacy of the NPS and make the organization a valuable, relevant piece of our national conversations.

Education and Youth

One of the strongest elements in the National Park Service's "Centennial Final Report," released in December 2016, is the directive to advance the NPS Education Mission. To do this, the NPS has set out a number of directives for itself. These include capturing the interest of the public and communicating with them effectively through social media and technology, collaborating with partners and education institutions to expand programs and use of parks, and strengthening the NPS as an education institution in general. The NPS's commitment to education serves not only to increase and enrich students' learning, but it helps to center and increase students' experiences of the national parks, potentially leading them to more highly value the outdoors. With this increased valuing, hopefully, comes increased awareness of challenges and issues facing natural areas, such as climate change. Thus, a better-informed audience can tackle these issues in the future. The National Park Service fits into the larger puzzle of educating America's children on all subjects and contributes to America's educational landscape, but it also weaves the parks into the **consciousness**—awareness or perception—of youth in the United States, making sure that today's young people grow up with an understanding of "what's out there" and why and how we must protect it.

School groups are an important population for the NPS to engage as they pursue their education mission. They hope to help raise the next generation of nature-loving adults.

fact!

Delaware is the only state in the United States that does not have a national park or national monument.

In order to turn future teachers, voters, scientists, and policymakers into park lovers and conservationists, the NPS is working hard to attract young people to its parks and programs. Unfortunately, many young people have not heard of most national parks or don't know where they are! Increasing access for youth, especially those living in urban areas, is one of the NPS's goals for the next century. One of the main ways in which the NPS is working to accomplish important conservation work while building a love for the parks into our country's next generation is through the United States Youth Conservation Corps, or YCC. This is a summer youth employment program, usually about eight to ten weeks long, in which youth ages fifteen through eighteen complete meaningful work experiences in national parks, forests, wildlife refuges, and more. YCC members, not unlike the CCC workers of the 1930s, focus on building trails, cleaning up campgrounds, improving wildlife habitats, teaching environmental education to children, and preserving historic structures.

The NPS is also working to cultivate youth leadership and engage youth in science through the Biodiversity Youth Ambassador program. The program also helps to spread biodiversity awareness in communities and schools across the country. It allows students, chosen by the host park of the annual NPS/National Geographic Society BioBlitz, to become official Volunteers-in-Parks. The program itself is coordinated by the NPS in partnership with host parks, the families of park ambassadors,

This Biodiversity Youth Ambassador group is shown jumping for joy during a BioBlitz event in 2015.

This group of visitors rafts down the Colorado River at Grand Canyon National Park.

National Park, and opposition to development near Grand Canyon, Joshua Tree, and Glacier National Parks all exemplify large-scale, landscape-focused solutions.

The NPS continues to work on finding solutions to the many challenges facing the parks today. However, some of the most difficult challenges are of a size and scope that we cannot yet grasp. They are related to climate change.

What Lies Ahead

Now is the time to go out and discover the parks! Some of their most beautiful, natural wonders are currently threatened by environmental changes and budgetary restrictions, and may not be there forever. A day pass to a national park usually costs ten to fifteen dollars, but you may be eligible for a free annual pass from the NPS. Current US military members and their families can receive free passes to the parks. All fourth-grade students can obtain a free pass for the duration of their fourth-grade school year through the Every Kid in a Park program. An annual senior citizen pass costs twenty dollars, and an access pass is free for residents with permanent disabilities. Additionally, volunteers who have clocked at least 250 service hours of service with a federal agency are eligible for a free volunteer pass. Of course, if you don't fit into any of those categories, a regular annual pass can be had for just eighty dollars.

fact!

California and Alaska have the most national parks of any states in the United States. They each have eight parks dotting their unique landscapes.

That pass allows you to visit as many parks as you want, as many times as you want, during the year!

Over the course of its one-hundred-plus-year history, the NPS has continued to champion its mission of preserving the resources of the national park system for future generations. Though the agency has encountered challenges—world wars, budget shortfalls, waning visitors, booming visitor numbers, invasive species, and more—and battled environmental threats along the way, the NPS has stayed both afloat and atop the minds and hearts of all those who get the chance to visit the parks, work inside them, or benefit from any of their heritage areas, monuments, or programs. The effect of the NPS is far-reaching, touching lives outside of the park boundaries. Today, people of all ages and stages are encouraged to walk through the rustic park entrances, lace up their hiking boots, and experience the natural wonder and beauty of the parks. Each year, millions take that step, making amazing memories that will last well into the future.

Get Involved!

Have you ever wanted to work in a national park? Now is the time! Since 1957, the Student Conservation Association has been matching students with national parks, monuments, and wilderness areas in order to complete projects and become leaders in sustainability. The SCA is all about hands-on service learning. It offers many programs for people from ages fifteen to twenty-one and older.

The SCA's Conservation Crews program is best for younger students. It was modeled after the Civilian Conservation Corps that grew out of the Great Depression. Conservation crews complete many different kinds of projects on the local, regional, and communal level. Trail building and maintenance, wildlife research, habitat restoration, and **GIS mapping** are just some of the activities for participants. Each person receives specialized training and valuable experience, and sometimes they are even eligible for professional certifications as part of these groups.

Many programs also offer stipends and academic credit. The SCA is an amazing way to get up close and personal with the outdoors, explore potential career options, and work with a community of conservation-minded youth who are all ready to learn new things, make friends, and explore the wilderness.

Glossary

biodiversity The variety of living organisms in a particular habitat or environment.

carbon footprint The amount of carbon dioxide released into the atmosphere due to the consumption of fossil fuels.

concessioner A private business that has a contract with the federal government that allows them to operate inside public parkland.

consciousness Awareness or perception.

conservation The act of preserving, protecting, or restoring the natural environment.

Dust Bowl A period of severe dust storms that damaged prairie areas in Oklahoma, Kansas, Arkansas, and northern Texas during the 1930s.

friends group A supportive organization that raises private funds for particular parks and projects.

gateway regions Areas that directly surround NPS sites.

GIS mapping A computer graphic information system (GIS) that captures, stores, checks, and displays data related to Earth's surface, all on one map.

native species Species of plants, animals, or other organisms that originate in the areas where they are found.

parkitecture Also known as "National Park Service Rustic," a style of architecture that developed within NPS parks in an effort to create appealing structures that fit into the landscape.

public good A service, or in this case a place, that is provided without exclusion.

purview The scope or limits of authority.

QR code A special type of barcode image, containing an array of black and white squares, that stores information that can be accessed by the camera on a smartphone.

ranger A worker who is entrusted with protecting and preserving the parklands.

stewardship The responsible planning and management of resources.

sustainability Avoidance of the depletion of natural resources, on a day-to-day basis, in order to maintain ecological balance.

Further Information

Books

Hansen, Heather. *Prophets and Moguls, Rangers and Rogues, Bison and Bears.* Seattle, WA: Mountaineers Books, 2015.

Luong, Q.T. *Treasured Lands: A Photographic Odyssey Through America's National Parks.* Petaluma, CA: Cameron + Company, 2016.

Moor, Robert. *On Trails: An Exploration.* New York: Simon & Schuster, 2016.

White, Mel. *National Geographic Complete National Parks of the United States.* 2nd edition. Washington, DC: National Geographic, 2016.

Websites

Find a Park

https://www.nps.gov/findapark/index.htm

This website, maintained by the National Park Service, is your one-stop shop for finding a nearby national park or planning a cross-country road trip.

Video Wall

https://www.nps.gov/subjects/youthprograms/video-wall.htm

This page offers a selection of short videos—all made by youth—that demonstrates how teens and kids are active within the national parks.

Youth Conservation Corps

https://www.nps.gov/subjects/youthprograms/ycc.htm

This website details the Youth Conservation Corps.

Organizations

National Parks Conservation Association

https://www.npca.org

This organization works to advocate on behalf of the national parks. Visit this site to learn more about what they do.

National Park Foundation

https://www.nationalparks.org

The official fundraising group of the national parks, the National Park Foundation, also helps fund initiatives in individual parks.

National Park Service

http://www.nps.gov

Visit the official website of the National Park Service.

Bibliography

Albright, Horace M. *Creating the National Park Service: The Missing Years*. Norman, Oklahoma: University of Oklahoma Press. 1999.

Anderson, Joel, and Nathan Anderson. *59 Illustrated National Parks*. Nashville, TN: Anderson Design Group, Inc., 2016.

Benton-Short, Lisa. *The National Mall: No Ordinary Public Space*. Toronto, Canada: University of Toronto Press, 2016.

Burns, Ken, and Dayton Duncan. *The National Parks: America's Best Idea*. New York: Alfred A. Knopf, 2009.

Corapi, Sarah. "150 years ago, Abraham Lincoln signed the Yosemite Grant Act." *PBS.org*, June 30, 2014. http://www.pbs.org/newshour/rundown/yosemite-turns-150.

Eilperin, Juliet. "National Parks Face Severe Funding Crunch." *Washington Post*, August 19, 2012. https://www.washingtonpost.com/national/health-science/national-parks-face-severe-funding-crunch/2012/08/19/959da5b0-e7ab-11e1-a3d2-2a05679928ef_story.html?utm_term=.170091c378c7.

Gajanan, Mahita. "Two More National Parks Appear to Defy Donald Trump on Twitter." *Time*, January 25, 2017. http://time.com/4649608/national-parks-climate-change-donald-trump-tweets.

Hansen, Heather. *Prophets and Moguls, Rangers and Rogues, Bison and Bears*. Seattle, WA: Mountaineers Books, 2015.

Hetter, Katia. "A Salute to Oldest U.S. National Parks: Yellowstone, Yosemite, Rainier, Others." *CNN*, April 23, 2017. http://www.cnn.com/travel/article/national-park-service-history-first-sites-feat/index.html.

Matchar, Emily. "Five Ways National Parks Are Embracing Technology." *Smithsonian*, August 1, 2016. http://www.smithsonianmag.com/innovation/five-ways-national-parks-are-embracing-technology-180959970.

National Park Service. US Department of the Interior. https://www.nps.gov/index.htm.

Repanshek, Kurt. "President's Budget Proposal Viewed as Overly Harsh for National Parks." *National Parks Traveler*, March 16, 2017. https://www.nationalparkstraveler.com/2017/03/presidents-budget-proposal-viewed-overly-harsh-national-parks.

Zaslowsky, Dyan. *These American Lands*. New York: Henry Holt and Company, Inc., 1987.

Index

Page numbers in **boldface** are illustrations. Entries in **boldface** are glossary terms.

About the Author

Kaitlyn Duling believes in the power of words to change hearts, minds, and, ultimately, actions. A poet, nonfiction author, and grant writer who grew up in Illinois, she now resides in Pittsburgh, Pennsylvania, where she works aboard a bookmobile for Reading Is Fundamental Pittsburgh and helps kids learn to love to read. She knows that knowledge of the past is the key to the future, and wants to make certain that all children and families have access to high-quality information.